Tail Call Optimization

Efficient Programming Techniques

Table of Contents

Chapter 1. Introduction

Special Report: Embarking on the Journey towards Efficient Programming with Tail Call Optimization

In the vast landscape of computer programming, numerous techniques lie waiting for developers, programmers, and software enthusiasts to discover, each offering unique opportunities to refine their coding skills. One such gem, brimming with potential for efficiency, is Tail Call Optimization (TCO). This Special Report takes a careful, down-to-earth approach to delve into the heart of TCO. We intricately weave the principles and workings of this highly technical concept into comprehensible sections, suitable for both seasoned coders and novices alike. Armed with practical examples and hindsight of experts, the report unravels the transformative role TCO can play in coding paradigms, unlocking the doors to a highly efficient, less resource-intensive programming world. Welcome aboard this enlightening journey - it's time to declutter the stacks and get optimizing!

Chapter 2. Demystifying Tail Call Optimization: An Introduction

Prior to diving deep into the realm of Tail Call Optimization (TCO), we need to arm ourselves with an understanding of the bedrock on which it stands: the function call. Functions comprise the building blocks of any program, no matter how simple or complex. They encapsulate a set of instructions designed to perform a specific task. Once a function is invoked, it's layered onto the call stack, a resource instrumental in helping track the execution context of functions. Only when a function finishes executing does it vacate the stack, giving room for the next function to execute. This hand-off is smooth and uneventful until we face a prolific chain of function calls a.k.a recursive function calls. The burgeoning tower of such calls on the stack can lead to its overflowing, causing the infamous 'stack overflow', a fatal event that results in the crashing of a program.

2.1. The Essence of Recursion

Braided into the DNA of numerous algorithms, recursion is a potent programming methodology. It can elegantly express solutions to complex problems such as traversing data structures (binary trees, linked lists, etc.), implementing the Fibonacci series, Tower of Hanoi, factorials, and more. Typically, a recursive function calls itself directly or indirectly within its body until it reaches a base case, catalyzing the extrication from the recursive spiral. Yet this constant hoarding of function invocations on the call stack is inclined to push the stack space to its brink.

Consider the following function designed to compute the factorial of a number:

```
function factorial(n) {
  if (n === 0) return 1;
  return n * factorial(n - 1);
}
```

The factorial function continually calls itself until it reaches the base case (n=0). During this process, each function invocation is pushed onto the stack. This seemingly harmless function could lead to trouble when 'n' becomes a large number, putting tremendous pressure on the stack space.

2.2. Enter Tail Call Optimization

A path to mitigate the stack overflow peril and enhance efficiency is trailing our discussion so far. This path is paved by TCO, a concept embraced by several modern programming languages including Scheme, Lua, Elixir, and certain versions of JavaScript (via strict mode in ECMAScript 6 i.e., ES6). By leveraging TCO, a recursive function can be converted into a loop, eliminating the risk of stack overflow.

But what precisely is a tail call? In essence, a tail call is a function call that's the final action of another function. The function has nothing else left to do except return the result of the invoked function. To qualify for TCO, the function call must reside in the 'tail position', i.e., it's the last operation performed in a function.

Rewriting our factorial function using a tail call now:

```
function factorial(n, acc = 1) {
  if (n === 0) return acc;
  return factorial(n - 1, n * acc);
}
```

The rewritten function now bears a second argument, 'acc', an accumulator storing multiplication results along the recursion. Once the base case is bumped into, the accumulated result is returned, avoiding piling recursive calls onto the stack.

2.3. The Magic of Tail Call Optimization

How does TCO work its magic? The secret recipe is in recognizing when a tail call is in effect. The compiler or interpreter observes this and instead of layering new function calls onto the stack, it merely adjusts the inputs to the existing function execution. This process is termed as 'frame reuse'. The action directly contributes to reducing memory consumption, boosting the efficiency of the program, and eliminating worries about stack overflows.

In essence, TCO morphs recursive procedures into iteration, maintaining their elegance while dodging the potential dangers of recursion. It's like having your cake and eating it too!

2.4. Caveats and Considerations

While TCO sounds exquisite, it may not derive the same level of support from all programming languages. Not all languages are designed to handle TCO, and amongst those that do, the degree of support varies. For instance, ES6, the sixth edition of JavaScript specification, embraces TCO only under strict mode. However, even this has not been adopted universally by all browsers due to performance implications. Additionally, some language environments offer explicit mechanisms to enable TCO, requiring the developer to be cognizant and diligent while using this optimization strategy.

In conclusion, TCO isn't a magic wand that functions autonomously.

It requires a deep understanding of recursion, the role of the call stack, and a conscious effort during implementation – basked in these insights, you are well on your way to capitalizing on the immense potential of Tail Call Optimization.

Chapter 3. Building Blocks of Computer Programming and Recursion

To take the first leap in our journey towards understanding tail call optimization, let's travel into the core of computer programming and strip down its building blocks. At the same time, we'll discover the concept of recursion, a technique so intimately related to the use of TCO.

Every piece of code, no matter how intricate or expansive, can eventually be dismantled into a simple set of building blocks. These basic elements work together in amazing harmony to create comprehensive programs that solve myriad complex problems. Let's take a closer look.

3.1. Variables and Data Types

A variable is a symbolic name given to some known or unknown quantity or information, for the sake of reference or analyzing. Variables in programming are an embodiment of this concept. They are the fundamental means by which data is stored and manipulated in a program. Data types, on the other hand, are specific kinds of data items, characterized by the interpretations that the programming language assigns to the data. Common data types include integers, floating-point numbers, characters, strings, and arrays.

```
var stringVariable = "Hello, World!";
var numberVariable = 888;
```

In the above example, `stringVariable` is a string data type holding the value "Hello, World!", whereas `numberVariable` is an integer data type containing the value 888.

3.2. Control Structures

Control Structures guide the order in which the statements in a program get executed. They play a significant role in decision making, looping, and branching in a program. The three basic types of control structures include sequential, selection (decision making), and repetition (iteration).

1. Sequential: In sequential control structure, the statements are executed in order.

2. Selection: In selection control structure, a condition is evaluated first, if the condition is true, one set of statements are executed otherwise the other set is executed.

3. Repetition: In repetition control structure, a sequence of code is executed until a certain condition is met.

3.3. Functions and Procedures

Functions and Procedures are the modular building blocks of structured programming. These small modules of code can be called, or invoked, from any part of the program, enabling code reuse and enhanced readability.

```
function addNumbers(x, y) {
  return x + y;
}


console.log(addNumbers(5, 3));  // Outputs: 8
```

In the above example, `addNumbers` is a function that takes two parameters (x and y) and returns their sum.

Having laid out the basic building blocks of programming, let's pivot to a fascinating aspect of function invocation — recursion.

Recursion is the process of solving problems by breaking them down into smaller and smaller sub-problems until we get to a small enough problem that it can be solved trivially. In programming, a recursive function is one that calls itself during its execution, working its way incrementally to the problem's solution.

Consider the common programming challenge of calculating the factorial of a number, where the factorial function (often symbolized by an exclamation point) multiplies every integer from the given number down to one. Using recursion, the simple solution would be:

```
function factorial(n) {
  if (n === 0) {
    return 1;
  } else {
    return n * factorial(n - 1);
  }
}


console.log(factorial(5));  // Outputs: 120
```

In the function above, when calculating factorial(5), it breaks the problem into a smaller, simpler problem: 5 * factorial(4). The function continues breaking down the problem until it reaches factorial(0), which returns 1 (the base case). Once the base case is reached, the function can then successively return and solve the higher levels of the problem, one at a time.

While the process of recursion can often simplify complex problems, it can result in the consuming of a lot of computational resources and memory. This happens because each function call gets its own space on the stack - a part of computer memory where all the magic of function execution happens. With complex and deep recursion, the stack can get filled up fast, affecting the system's performance.

This is where our efficiency-enhancer, Tail Call Optimization, comes into the picture. But, before we dive into that, it is important that we understand stack frames and call stacks, which will be our next stop in this enlightening journey.

With solid ground covered in terms of programming basics and an understanding of recursion, we are geared to embark on the next step - introducing and understanding Tail Call Optimization. Stay tuned for our deep-dive into TCO and its transformative potential for the programming world.

Chapter 4. Deep Dive into Function Calls and Stack Frames

Before we delve into the profound realm of Tail Call Optimization (TCO), it is quintessential to lay the foundational understanding of function calls and stack frames. This vista of programming we are about to explore forms the bedrock in understanding the workings of TCO.

4.1. Understanding Function Calls

In the ambit of computer programming, functions or procedures are fundamental building blocks. When we discuss function calls, we simply refer to the act of invoking these blocks of reusable code - a deeply embedded concept within the programming scheme.

In high-level programming languages, whenever a function is called, there are a series of steps that take place, generally bucketed into two main processes:

1. The control is transferred from the calling function (the caller) to the called function (the callee).

2. Once the execution of the callee is complete, the control is reverted back to the caller.

Although it might seem straightforward, there's much more at play under the hood. It's more than just the action of calling a function — it involves setting up the environment for the function execution, preserving the current execution state of the program, and managing the values of variables and parameters. All this multitude of actions ensures the smooth and correct functioning of the program.

4.2. Unfolding Stack Frames

To carry out operations related to function calls, computer programs use a region of computer's memory, commonly referred to as the 'Call Stack'. A Stack, by its design, is a Last-In-First-Out (LIFO) data structure, which grows and shrinks dynamically, perfectly fitting for managing function calls and their respective scope.

When a function is called, a corresponding unit known as a 'stack frame' or 'activation record' gets appended on top of the call stack. This often results from a combination of steps including:

1. Saving the return address: The address in the caller where the execution should resume post the callee's execution - effectively a bookmark in the execution path of the program.

2. Pushing arguments: The arguments passed to the function are pushed onto the stack.

3. Saving frame pointers: This allows the program to know where the frame starts in the stack.

4. Space for local variables: This is required for maintaining their values during function execution.

Each stack frame embodies the complete execution context of the function it corresponds to. This context encapsulates the return address, passed parameters, local variables, and other temporary data that the function might require during its execution.

The LIFO nature facilitates a clean handling of recursive function calls, as each invocation creates its own new context without interfering with the data of any previous calls. Therefore, recursion is enabled and made possible by the use of the stack and its management.

4.3. Anatomy of a Stack Frame

Let's dissect a typical stack frame for further understanding. The structure presented here is a generalized one and the actual layout might differ based on the language, compiler, or the machine architecture.

Here's an abstracted view of a stack frame:

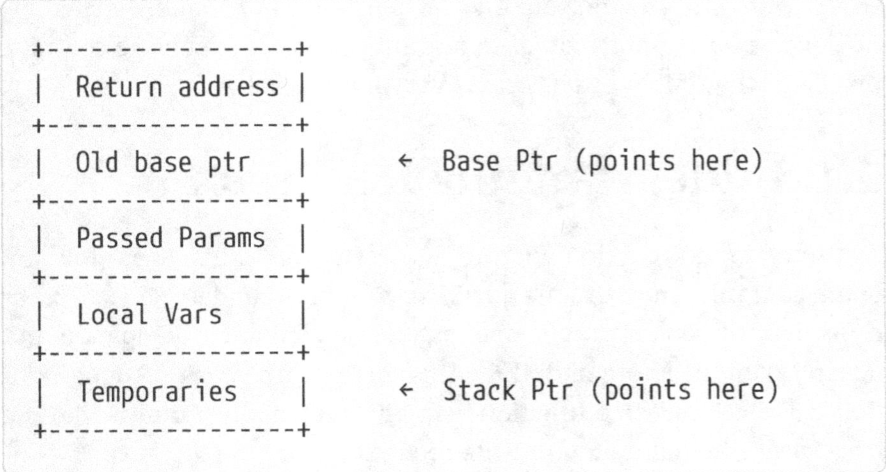

The Stack Pointer (SP) always points to the top of the stack (the last inserted element), and the Base Pointer (BP), also known as the frame pointer, points to the base of the current stack frame.

As we move from one function call to another, the BP and SP adjust dynamically to reflect the top and bottom of the current stack frame, helping manage recursive and nested function calls efficiently.

From the foundation laid in this chapter, we understand the 'what' and 'why' behind function calls and stack frames. In future chapters, we'll draw from these basics to unravel the enigmatic nature of Tail Call Optimization and unleash its true potential.

Chapter 5. The Concept of Recursion in Depth

Every serious engagement with programming languages eventually leads to grappling with a powerful but sometimes befuddling concept: recursion. In its simplest definition, recursion in programming is a process in which a function calls itself as a subroutine. This might seem an unusual, even improbable structure; however, recursion provides an elegant approach to solving complex problems that might otherwise be very hard to solve.

5.1. Understanding Recursion

To understand recursion, picture a set of nested dolls. Each doll you open contains another one just like it, only smaller. This process repeats until you reach the smallest doll, which can't be opened and doesn't contain another doll. In this analogy, the task of opening a doll is like a recursive function call, and the smallest doll is like the base case—the point at which the recursion ends.

In the programming world, a recursive function solves a problem by solving smaller instances of the same problem. The base case is typically a condition wherein the function does not call itself, thereby avoiding an infinite loop of calls. Thereby, every recursive function consists of at least one base case and one recursive case.

Consider this simple example, a function in Python that computes the factorial of a number:

```python
def factorial(n):

    # Base case: 1 factorial is itself.
    if n == 1:
```

```
      return 1

    # Recursive case: n factorial is n times (n-1)
  factorial.
    else:
        return n * factorial(n-1)
```

In this function, the base case is when n equals 1. The recursive case is the function call factorial(n-1). The function multiplies n by the result of the recursive case, leading to the expected result for the factorial of n.

5.2. Visualizing Call Stacks in Recursion

An excellent way to understand recursion and its intricacies is to visualize the call stack. When a recursive function is called, each call waits for the return value of the subsequent call before it can return a value. These waiting calls are stacked up, akin to stack data structure, where the last function call made is the first to resolve, akin to the LIFO (Last In First Out) principle.

Given a code factorial(5); based on the example above, the call stack sequence would look something like this:

```
--> factorial(5)
    --> factorial(4)
        --> factorial(3)
            --> factorial(2)
                --> factorial(1)
Returns 1
              <-- 2*1
          <-- 3*2
      <-- 4*6
```

```
<-- 5*24 = 120
```

This visualization elucidates that each subsequent call waits for the return value before it can process and return a value. The process can consume a significant stack space for a more significant number, which can lead to a stack overflow error. This shortcoming is precisely where Tail Call Optimization (TCO) comes in to minimize stack use and optimize function calls.

5.3. Differences Between Recursion and Iteration

While recursion and iteration are both strategies to solve programming problems through repeated execution of a set of instructions, they differ in their mechanism and resource usage.

Iterations repeat through a loop, creating a single call frame in the memory stack, executing the entire process within this frame. Iterations are memory efficient but, at times, create less elegant and more verbose code.

Recursion, in contrast, uses multiple call frames, one for each recursive call. This repeated piling can lead to more memory use, and in severe cases, stack overflow. On the bright side, recursion can simplify solutions for complex problems, resulting in more intuitive and cleaner code.

Consider a simple function to calculate the nth number in the Fibonacci sequence. The iterative and recursive solutions would look something like this:

Iterative solution:

```
def fibonacci_iterative(n):
```

```python
    a, b = 0, 1
    for _ in range(n):
        a, b = b, a + b
    return a
```

Recursive solution:

```python
def fibonacci_recursive(n):
    if n <= 1:
        return n
    else:
        return fibonacci_recursive(n-1) +
fibonacci_recursive(n-2)
```

While the iterative version uses a simple loop to add up values, the recursive version breaks the problem down into smaller steps. Besides, the recursive function poses a real risk of stack overflow for high values of n.

5.4. Advantages and Disadvantages of Using Recursion

Recursion packs a powerful punch in problem-solving. Its logic is simple, leading to cleaner and readable code. It's highly effective for solving complex problems that can be broken down into smaller, identical problems, including sorting algorithms like Merge Sort and Quick Sort, divide and conquer algorithms, tree, and graph traversal, to name a few.

On the flip side, recursion's major drawback lies in its memory usage. Each recursive call adds a layer to the call stack, and for scenarios where function calls are immense, the memory stack may run out, resulting in an overflow. Furthermore, it might not be as intuitive to think in a recursive way, for those new to the concept, adding a potential debugging challenge.

5.5. Conclusion

Recursion might seem a daunting concept at first, but once the fundamental mechanism is cleaved, it turns out to be an elegant approach to complex problem-solving. Packed with potential, recursion's wizardry lies in problem simplification, powering through programming challenges with pared-down clarity. The memory issue, significant yet surmountable, paves the way for exploring Tail Call Optimization(TCO), to smoothen the recursive ride. A balanced blend of understanding recursion and its optimization strategies can make for a phenomenal programming repertoire. Now that we have immersed ourselves in recursion, the next logical excursion takes us to TCO – a leap towards high-efficiency programming universe.

Chapter 6. Tail Calls: A Closer Examination

Tail calls play an irreplaceable role in the realm of modern computer programming, thanks to their inherent ability to make recursion manageable and maintain the system resources. A tail call is essentially a subroutine call performed as the final action of another subroutine. If a call to a subroutine is the last action, it makes its parent subroutine a tail call. This raises a pertinent question - why should it matter if the subroutine call is the last action or not? Isn't a subroutine call just a subroutine call? As the discussion progresses, you will discover just how pivotal this distinction can be when it comes to efficient programming.

6.1. Understanding the Nature of Stack Frames

Before delving into the detailed workings of tail calls, one must first understand the nature of 'stack frames.' When you call a subroutine, the computer must "remember" the place in the code where it needs to return after executing the subroutine. It also needs to remember the state of all local variables at the point of the call. This is achieved through a data structure called a stack frame. A stack frame is created for every subroutine call and is stored in the system stack.

Now, imagine a situation where a subroutine call is the last action in the code. Here, the system is about to leave the current stack frame, meaning all local variables will be unwound, and the system will never need to return to this stack frame. In essence, the current stack frame has served its purpose and can be cleaned up: it is a tail call.

6.2. Recursive Calls and Stack Overflow

Recursive calls, without the ambit of tail call optimization, significantly increase the risk of a stack overflow. A recursive function is one that addresses a problem by solving smaller instances of the same problem. Classical examples include factorial or Fibonacci sequence calculations, both of which involve a function calling itself.

Without tail call optimization, recursive calls accumulate on the stack, each awaiting a return to complete their calculations. This accumulation can quickly lead to a stack overflow error. But what if there is a method to recycle the current function's stack frame for a subsequent function call? This is where tail calls shine.

6.3. Working Mechanism of Tail Calls

When a tail call scenario happens, important memory optimizations can be carried out. Since the parent function has finished its operations and needs only to return the child function's result, there is no need to maintain the parent function's stack frame. Thus, the child function can reuse (or overwrite) the parent function's stack frame, which dramatically reduces the stack memory usage, especially in recursive calls.

In practical terms, a recursive tail call function will run with a constant space complexity of $O(1)$, as opposed to a non-optimized recursive function, which normally runs with a space complexity of $O(n)$.

6.4. Distinction Between Tail Calls and Non-Tail Calls

A critical factor that distinguishes tail calls from non-tail calls is whether the return value of any function f that calls another function g is used for any operation in f other than returning the value. Should any further computation be required, such as addition or division, or should the returned value need to be passed to another function for further processing, then this is not a tail call.

To be clear, please consider the following pseudocode:

```
function f(...) {
    ...
    return g(...);
}
```

In the example above, it is a tail call since the only operation f performs on the result of g(...) is to return it. However, consider this example:

```
function f(...) {
    ...
    return g(...) + h(...);
}
```

In this case, f requires the results of both g(...) and h(...), applies a further operation (addition), and returns the result. Hence, this is not a tail call.

6.5. Identifying and Write Tail Recursive Functions

For a function to take advantage of tail call optimization, it needs to be tail recursive, i.e., the recursion call should be in the tail position in the function. This might sometimes require rethinking and reformatting of the algorithm to ensure the recursive call comes last.

This can be exemplified by rewriting a function to compute factorials. The typical recursive implementation of a factorial function is not tail recursive:

```
function factorial(n) {
    if (n == 0) {
        return 1;
    } else {
        return n * factorial(n-1);
    }
}
```

In this example, the multiplication with n is the last operation. This code cannot take advantage of tail call optimization. To rewrite it as a tail recursive function, an accumulator variable is introduced:

```
function factorial(n, accumulator = 1) {
    if (n == 0) {
        return accumulator;
    } else {
        return factorial(n-1, n*accumulator);
    }
}
```

Now, the last operation of each function invocation (when n > 0) is the recursive call to factorial(), allowing for tail call optimization.

6.6. Languages Supporting Tail Call Optimizations

While tail call optimization greatly improves efficiency, particularly with recursive programming, not all programming languages support it. Languages that are frequently used for functional programming, such as Scheme, Lisp, Erlang, and Haskell, have robust TCO support, as recursion is a highly-utilized paradigm in functional programming.

Other languages, like Python, have refrained from implementing TCO, in part due to concerns about tracebacks in debugging and preserving relevant state information. JavaScript had it implemented as a part of ES6 standard, but as of now, it is implemented reliably solely in Safari. Languages like Java, C#, Swift, and Kotlin, meanwhile, do not inherently support TCO, but you can usually perform TCO manually with the keen use of iterative looping constructs.

In this chapter, we have taken a deeper look at tail calls, how they function in different coding scenarios, their relation to the efficient composition of recursive functions, and the benefits they offer in terms of memory usage. Recognizing a tail call and knowing how to leverage its capacity to optimize memory will all boil down to a programmer's comprehension of this powerful functional programming concept. Going forward, the importance of tail calls and tail call optimization is only likely to increase, and it behooves all programmers to familiarize themselves with, and master this important tool in their coding arsenal.

Chapter 7. Understanding Tail Call Optimization: A Shift in Perspective

A change of perspective is vital when probing tail call optimization (TCO). For the uninitiated, a tail call happens when a function's last operation is calling another function and nothing else. The elegance of this method lies in its potential for resource optimization.

When we aim to maximize the efficiency and minimize the resource usage of our code, each step we make towards better understanding and implementing TCO is invaluable. Understanding TCO requires a shift from conventional programming mindset to one that is more strategic and perceptive.

7.1. Getting Acquainted with Tail Calls

Imagine a scenario where we have a function A that calls function B in its last operation. This is a typical instance of a tail call. The implication here is that when function B finishes executing, the runtime does not need to return to function A, as there are no other operations left to be resolved. Hence, there is no need to maintain the stack frame of function A in the stack, making the tail call a more memory-efficient operation than a standard function call.

```
def function_a(x):
    result_b = function_b(x)
    return result_b
```

In the above Python snippet, the call to `function_b(x)` is not a tail call.

After calling `function_b(x)`, function A still has to return the result after being called. Contrastingly, see the below example of a tail call in Scheme, a dialect of Lisp, which supports TCO.

```
(define (rec_factorial n acc)
  (if (= n 0)
      acc
      (rec_factorial (- n 1) (* n acc)))))
```

Here, the recursive call to `rec_factorial` is a tail call. Once this call is made, there's no other operation left to be done in the calling function.

7.2. Meeting Tail Call Optimization (TCO)

The beauty of tail calls is amplified when we introduce the concept of TCO. This is a technique where the compiler or interpreter reuses the stack frame of the terminating function in the case of a tail call, minimizing or eliminating stack overflows in recursive calls.

In terms of how TCO works, imagine a function 'X' that, as its final action, calls function 'Y'. In a non-optimized scenario, this sequence would follow these steps:

- Start executing function X
- Stop executing function X
- Preserve the context of function X (creating a return point)
- Start executing function Y
- Stop executing function Y
- Restore the context of function X

- Continue execution from the preserved context

In TCO, the last three steps can be omitted. The context of function X is not required after function Y is called – this is the crux of TCO. Thus, the compiler or interpreter can repurpose the stack frame of function X for function Y.

This approach prevents the common pitfall of a stack overflow when dealing with recursive function calls – an issue encountered when memory is exhausted due to an excessive number of nested function calls occupying stack space. By adopting TCO, the stack doesn't grow with the number of recursive calls.

7.3. TCO in Different Languages

Interestingly, not all programming languages support TCO. Some languages such as Scheme mandate TCO; others like Python and Java do not support it. Each language employs specific optimization strategies, and the presence or absence of TCO can greatly affect how we write recursive functions.

For languages that don't support TCO (like Python), the programmer has to be careful with recursion depths or iterate explicitly using loops to prevent stack overflows. In Java, the JVM doesn't handle tail recursion efficiently either, and recursive procedures may also lead to a `StackOverflowError`.

Conversely, languages such as Scheme, Haskell, and Erlang support TCO and even promote a functional programming style that leverages recursion over iteration. In such languages, tail recursion is used extensively, ensuring memory efficiency.

7.4. Adapting Your Programming Style for TCO

Understanding TCO can foster a cognitive shift in coding practices - we can begin to see the 'solution' not just as the end-goal, but also the process of seamlessly fitting together smaller, more manageable pieces. To make optimal use of TCO, one has to practice and refine the technique of writing recursive functions as tail calls.

Yet, it's necessary to remember that while TCO offers a promising pathway towards more efficient code, indiscriminate use can lead to hard-to-understand code. Tall calls, when implemented without careful planning, can easily befuddle other developers or even your future self. Each coding process needs balance and precision. As with any advanced concept, the key is to learn judicious use.

Chapter 8. Epilogue: An Evolving Journey

Tail Call Optimization, rightly understood and applied, is a formidable tool in the hands of seasoned programmers and a potential game-changer for beginners. It offers profound benefits for particular applications, especially where deep recursion is required and languages that support TCO.

Learning TCO is not just about learning a new concept; it's an invitation to view the programming landscape from a more nuanced perspective. With every little switch in understanding and each technique added to your toolkit, the programming journey evolves, unveiling fresh vistas of coding prowess.

As the adage goes, the best time to have discovered TCO was the moment you entered the programming world; the second best time is now. With TCO, the path lies open to more efficient, cleaner, and less resource-intensive code. So, unburdened by the fear of stack overflows, you can harness recursion's power to the fullest, making the most out of your coding endeavor. Happy optimizing!

Chapter 9. Implementation of Tail Call Optimization in Various Programming Languages

Let's commence the journey by looking at how TCO is implemented in a variety of widely-known programming languages.

9.1. Understanding Recursion

Before delving into specific programming languages, it's best to establish a solid understanding of recursion, the cornerstone of TCO. In programming, recursion is a method where a function calls itself as its subroutine, exhibiting a self-referential nature.

```
function factorial(n) {
    if(n === 0) {
        return 1;
    }
    else {
        return n * factorial(n-1);
    }
}
```

In this JavaScript factorial function example, when a non-zero number is input, the function will continuously call itself, reducing the input by one each time, until it reaches zero. This recursive behavior can be optimized using TCO, which we'll explore next.

9.2. Tail Call Optimization in Scheme

Scheme, as a beacon of functional programming, has built-in TCO. It's one of only a few languages required by their standard to have this kind of optimization. Let's analyze a simple factorial function in Scheme:

```scheme
(define (factorial n)
    (define (iter product counter)
        (if (= counter 0)
            product
            (iter (* product counter) (- counter 1))))
    (iter 1 n))
```

Unlike our JavaScript function, this Scheme function is already optimized for TCO. The key here is in the inner `iter` function. Here, there is no computation after the recursive call to `iter`, thus it is a tail call. Therefore, the interpreter doesn't need to allocate additional stack frames for these recursive calls, and can simply "jump" directly to the recursive call, using constant stack space.

9.3. Tail Call Optimization in JavaScript

Modern JavaScript engines like Google's V8 (Node.js and Chrome) had experimental support for TCO via the 'harmony' flag. However, due to complications surrounding debugging semantics, proper tail calls (PTC) were not made officially part of the language specification (ECMAScript).

Yet, recursive functions can still take advantage of TCO by refactoring into a tail-recursive style, similar to the Scheme example:

```
function factorial(n) {
    function iter(product, counter) {
        if(counter === 0) {
            return product;
        }
        else {
            return iter(product * counter, counter - 1);
        }
    }
    return iter(1, n);
}
```

Despite the absence of automatic TCO, this form of tail recursion allows programmers to manually optimize their code, and minimize the risks associated with deep recursion levels, like stack overflow.

9.4. Tail Call Optimization in Python

Python, an imperatively styled language, has traditionally shunned built-in TCO. Guido van Rossum, Python's creator, has openly dismissed the addition of TCO. Python emphasizes readability and simplicity, and automatic TCO can obscure a program's explicit flow control.

However, TCO can still be effectively implemented using decorators and exceptions, harnessing Python's exception handling mechanism and powerful decorators:

```
def tail_recursive(f):
    CONTINUE = object()
    def decorated(*args, **kwargs):
        result = CONTINUE
        while result is CONTINUE:
            try:
```

```
                result = f(*args, **kwargs)
            except Recurse as r:
                args = r.args
                kwargs = r.kwargs
                result = CONTINUE
        return result
    return decorated


class Recurse(Exception):
    def __init__(self, *args, **kwargs):
        self.args = args
        self.kwargs = kwargs


@tail_recursive
def factorial(n, acc=1):
    return acc if n == 0 else Recurse(n-1, n*acc)
```

In this example, if the tail-recursive function wants to recurse, it raises the Recurse exception, which triggers another loop inside the decorator until the result is found.

9.5. Tail Call Optimization in Haskell

Finally, we have Haskell, another flagship of functional programming. Haskell, by default, uses TCO in its computations. It's a prime example of how TCO maintains performance in heavily recursive, functional programming:

```
factorial n = fact 1 n
    where
        fact acc 0 = acc
        fact acc n = fact (acc * n) (n-1)
```

Haskell uses guards instead of if-else statements. Like the other examples, no computation happens after the recursive call to `fact`, so this function is TCO-friendly.

9.6. Wrapping Up

As we have examined TCO in several languages, we see how differently each language implements the optimization. From inbuilt TCO support in languages such as Scheme and Haskell to those which do not support it directly like Python and JavaScript, but offer ways to leverage it using idioms of the language itself. Being adept at tail recursion and understanding how to leverage it in different programming environments can enhance efficiency and open doors to new programming methods and paradigms.

Chapter 10. The Benefits and Limitations of Tail Call Optimization

As developers, we are always on the lookout for the next step to make our programs run faster and cleaner – tail call optimization (TCO) offers a pathway to this goal. As with all techniques, however, it is critical to understand its advantages and limitations.

10.1. What is Tail Call Optimization?

Before diving into the benefits and limitations of TCO, we must understand what it is. In simple terms, TCO is an optimization technique used by compilers and interpreters to recycle the stack frame in a recursive function call if the recursive call is the final operation in a function. This occurs when a function's return value is a direct result of another function call. The 'tail' semantics is attributable to the situation where the recursive call happens at the end (tail) of the function or procedure.

10.2. Benefits of Tail Call Optimization

There are several compelling reasons to use TCO, and understanding these benefits can enrich our understanding of its practical applications:

1. *Improves Memory Efficiency* - The primary advantage of TCO is its ability to drastically reduce memory usage. Regular recursive calls result in nested stack frames, thus consuming a significant amount of memory. When using TCO, however, the stack frames

are recycled, which means that the memory overhead for function calls becomes a constant regardless of the recursion depth.

2. *Stack Overflow Mitigation* - Programs with heavy recursion are susceptible to a 'stack overflow,' which occurs when the call stack pointer exceeds the stack bound. This situation is particularly true for algorithms that implement deep recursion. By utilizing TCO, the possibility of stack overflow is mitigated because TCO reduces the space complexity from linear to constant.

3. *Performance Enhancement* - As TCO frees memory space substantially, it follows that it positively impacts the performance of programs by reducing book-keeping overhead typically required in function calls. The reuse of stack frames eliminates the need for push and pop operations for every call, thus enhancing runtime performance.

10.3. Limitations of Tail Call Optimization

While the benefits of employing TCO are substantial, there are limitations, as well:

1. *Debugging Issues* - TCO can complicate the process of debugging. Since it reuses stack frames, it can obscure the flow of function calls. This obscurity can make it challenging to trace the path of execution in debuggers and error reports.

2. *Limited Language Support* - Not all programming languages or compilers support TCO. Among the major languages, only a few like Scheme, Scala, and Elixir offer robust support for TCO. Others like Python, Java, and some versions of JavaScript do not support TCO, limiting its usability in these environments.

3. *Restrictive Coding Style* - To reap the benefits of TCO, developers must ensure that the tail recursive call is the last action in a

function. It can result in a forced and less-intuitive style of programming that may compromise readability.

10.4. Understanding Context and Use Cases

The decision to use TCO rests heavily on the context and requirements of the use case. Recursive problems like Tree traversals, Depth-First Search (DFS), Fibonacci numbers, and algorithms relying on backtracking can hugely benefit from TCO due to their inherently recursive nature.

However, for cases like Binary Search or Merge Sort, where the problem cannot be modeled as a tail recursion, leveraging TCO would be technically impossible. Moreover, if your primary development language does not support TCO or if you are working on a program where readability is a higher priority than performance, foregoing the use of TCO might be a more reasonable approach.

In essence, deciding to use TCO during development is a trade-off that developers must decide on carefully. Understanding both its benefits and limitations aids this decision-making process. Armed with this knowledge, developers can meaningfully leverage TCO's strengths while mitigating its weaknesses to create high-performance and efficient code that stands the test of time.

In the pursuit of mastering TCO, it's crucial to remember that the journey of learning and implementing such techniques is a marathon, not a sprint – patience, practice, and a thorough understanding of the underlying principles are all vital to mastering TCO and reaping its benefits effectively. Happy optimizing!

Chapter 11. Practical Examples: Implementing Tail Call Optimization

Typically in functional programming, recursion is prevalent, but this strategy uses copious amounts of memory. Herein lies the value of tail call optimization (TCO), as it effectively solves the memory use problem. To demonstrate TCO, we will delve into practical examples involving various scenario comparisons. Moreover, we will include a couple of programming languages to illustrate this concept's broad applicability.

11.1. Recursion Without TCO

Before we demonstrate TCO, it's imperative to grasp how recursion works without it. Consider the classic factorial problem which calculates the factorial of a number n (denoted as n!). Without TCO, here's how the recursive solution would look in JavaScript:

```
function factorial(n) {
    if (n === 0) {
        return 1;
    } else {
        return n * factorial(n - 1);
    }
}
```

In this code, for every recursive call to 'factorial(n-1)', a new stack frame is created to hold the locally scoped variables while the recursion evaluates. Therefore, for larger inputs, the call stack can grow significantly, potentially causing a stack overflow error.

11.2. Factorial with TCO

For a finer grasp on TCO, let's rewrite the factorial function, this time applying TCO principles. TCO modifies the recursion so that the last operation is the recursive call, which allows us to keep the memory footprint constant irrespective of the number of recursive calls.

The JavaScript TCO version of the factorial function, using an accumulator (acc) to keep track of the result until that point, can be written as:

```
function factorial(n, acc = 1) {
    if (n === 0) {
        return acc;
    } else {
        return factorial(n - 1, n * acc);
    }
}
```

The main difference here is that there's no need to return to the current stack frame once the recursive call has been evaluated, and the engine can reuse the current stack frame for the next call, thus eliminating the risk of a stack overflow.

11.3. Fibonacci Series Without TCO

Let's observe another common recursive problem - calculating the nth number in a Fibonacci series. The traditional recursive solution in Python is as follows:

```
def fibonacci(n):
    if n <= 1:
        return n
    else:
```

```
    return fibonacci(n-1) + fibonacci(n-2)
```

This code is particularly inefficient as it creates a large number of redundant calculations, leading to a considerable load on the call stack and overall performance challenges.

11.4. Fibonacci Series with TCO

Now, let's see how we can optimize the fibonacci function. In the modified version, we'll continue to use an accumulator (in this case, two - acc1 and acc2). Let's write the TCO version in Python:

```python
def fibonacci(n, acc1=0, acc2=1):
    if n == 0:
        return acc1
    elif n == 1:
        return acc2
    else:
        return fibonacci(n-1, acc2, acc1 + acc2)
```

This version not only avoids the redundant computations of the non-TCO version, but it also only requires a constant amount of memory, thanks to TCO.

11.5. Conclusion

We have delved into the practical value of TCO and its effect on well-known programming constructs. Although exceedingly beneficial, it's crucial to note the language support for TCO. While languages such as Scheme and Haskell fully support TCO, others like Python and currently JavaScript lack the native support. However, through the proper use of additional parameters (or accumulators), we can emulate TCO even in such languages.

TCO has a clear and striking benefit: it curbs excessive resource consumption, specifically memory, paving the way for a more efficient coding strategy. Furthermore, it promotes the use of recursion, a generally cleaner, more concise and easier-to-understand construct than its iterative counterpart.

As coding paradigms shift towards more functional styles, TCO stands to grow in importance. Pioneering developers can make a significant impact on resource utilization and program efficiency by embracing and correctly implementing this principle. The next step in this journey would be to learn further optimization strategies and comprehend how they fit in your overall coding strategies. Let's continue this exciting journey of exploration and learning together!

Chapter 12. Tail Call Optimization: Future Trends and Applications

Efficient programming practices continue to evolve, and Tail Call Optimization (TCO) remains at the forefront of these emerging trends. Owing to its distinctive ability to streamline programs and ensure optimal resource usage, TCO has gathered significant attention in the development community. Its future appears promising, with substantial potential applications that can drive enhanced productivity and efficiency in the coding realm.

12.1. Understanding the Evolution towards TCO

The journey to efficient program optimization and TCO has been characterized by continuous learning and advancement. Initially, most programming languages didn't incorporate TCO because they were primarily centered on imperative programming. However, with the rise of functional programming paradigms, the benefits of TCO started to gain recognition. Languages that support functional programming have begun integrating TCO to tap into its potential for enabling more efficient, less resource-consuming code.

The evolution of the computing landscape, coupled with the need for higher performance at lower cost, further underlines the potential of TCO. As our world becomes increasingly data-centric, the demand for tightly optimized code that can handle resource-intensive operations without driving up costs will continue to grow.

12.2. TCO as an Efficiency Booster in High-level Languages

One major trend in TCO utilization can be observed in high-level programming languages. Notably, most of these languages, such as Python and JavaScript, do not inherently support TCO due to their emphasis on keeping the stack trace for potential debugging. But with modern development favoring leaner, more efficient code, the value of TCO in these contexts is increasingly apparent.

JavaScript, for example, introduced TCO in the 6th edition of ECMAScript, although implementation across engines has been varied. This was a significant step, as it marked the beginning of an essential shift in how common high-level languages consider TCO and its potential to optimize coding.

However, there's still a long way to go before mainstream adoption. JavaScript's case is instructive: although TCO support is part of the language specification, its actual implementation in real-world coding remains sparse due to challenges in backward compatibility and debugging.

12.3. TCO as an Aid in Resource-Intensive Applications

As software development trends towards high-performance applications involving data science, real-time computing, and concurrent systems, there is an increasing need for efficient memory utilization. Memory-related crashes present a significant risk, particularly in these multi-tasking environments where memory stack overflow can lead to system failure.

In this context, TCO has a critical role to play. By eliminating needless memory allocation and keeping the stack from overflowing, TCO can significantly contribute to the stability of high-load systems. There is still much to learn about the application of TCO in these domains, and continued future research will drive our understanding and effective use of this optimization technique.

12.4. Future Avenues and Challenges

The future of TCO is rich with possibilities, as its benefits become more widely recognized across the programming landscape. With further advancements in programming languages and decoding technologies, TCO can revolutionize the way code operates, driving efficiencies at the micro and macro levels.

At the same time, the road ahead is not without its challenges. Introducing TCO into a language that doesn't inherently support it can complicate debugging and potential backward compatibility. Consequently, there is a need for innovative solutions that balance the benefits of TCO with visibility into the stack trace, crucial for debugging processes.

Another concern is the lack of widespread knowledge and understanding among developers regarding TCO. This gap could limit the technique's adoption rate and complicates its implementation in teams unfamiliar with this optimization method. Hence, bridging this knowledge gap through quality technical education and resources will prove critical as we move towards wider TCO adoption.

Tail Call Optimization holds immense potential for future trends in coding. By reducing unnecessary memory consumption and enabling more efficient code, it opens new horizons for high-performance, cost-effective computing. As we forge ahead into a more data-driven, resource-conscious future, unlocking the full potential of TCO will be a transformational driver in the world of efficient programming.

www.ingramcontent.com/pod-product-compliance
Lightning Source LLC
Chambersburg PA
CBHW071035260726
48661CB00007B/3029